DISCOVERING THE TECHNOLOGY OF ANCIENT MESOPOTAMIA

LINDSEY LOWE

Cavendish Square

Published in 2024 by Cavendish Square Publishing, LLC
2544 Clinton Street, Buffalo, NY 14224

Portions of this work were originally authored by Charlie Samuels and published as *Technology in Ancient Mesopotamia*. All new material this edition authored by Lindsey Lowe.

Children's Publisher: Anne O'Daly
Design Manager: Keith Davis
Designer: Lynne Lennon
Picture Manager: Sophie Mortimer

Picture Credits
Front Cover: Shutterstock: Stefan Holm br, Krikkiat t.
Alamy: Ancient Art & Architecture 37; British Museum: 25; Dreamstime: Sophie James 40; iStock: 4, G. Genova 36; Public Domain: Ancient Oriental Museum Istanbul/Osama Shukir Muhammed Amim FRCP 43, Lasse Jensen 19; Shutterstock: 20, Aantonio Abrignani 9, 11, allamimages 13, AstralManSigmaDelta 22, Felix Friebe 24, Kamira 30, 31, mayk.75 10, Jerry Rainey 17, Styve Reineck 12, Opis Zagreb 8; Thinkstock: Dorling Kindersley RF 23, 26, 35, Hemera 28, 34; istockphoto 33; Photos.com 27, 29, 38; University of Chicago: Oriental Institute Museum/Anna R. Ressman 32.

Cataloging-in-Publication Data

Names: Lowe, Lindsey.
Title: Discovering the technology of ancient Mesopotamia / Lindsey Lowe.
Description: Buffalo, New York : Cavendish Square Publishing, 2024. I
Series: Discovering ancient technology I Includes glossary and index.
Identifiers: ISBN 9781502669452 (pbk.) I ISBN 9781502669469 (library bound) I
ISBN 9781502669476 (ebook)
Subjects: LCSH: Civilization, Assyro-Babylonian--Juvenile literature. I Iraq--History--To 634--
Juvenile literature. I Iraq--Civilization--To 634--Juvenile literature.
Classification: LCC DS69.5 L69 2024 I DDC 609.35--dc23

CPSIA compliance information: Batch #CSCSQ24: For further information contact Cavendish Square Publishing LLC at 1-877-980-4450.

Printed in the United States of America

CONTENTS

INTRODUCTION

The lion became the symbol of Babylon in the seventh century B.C.E., during the city's second major period of importance.

The ancient Mesopotamians lived in what is now Iraq. Through their inventiveness, they built the world's first urban culture. Although they lacked many important resources, such as wood and most metals, they had mud from the banks of the Tigris and Euphrates Rivers. They used this to make mud bricks and used them to build some of the world's first cities. They also created the world's first writing on clay tablets. Mud dries and crumbles over time, so few of their buildings remain. However, the influence of Mesopotamia is everywhere. They were the first people to use the wheel and invented the zodiac and one of the earliest calendars. They also learned to cast bronze and iron objects, and to make glass.

BETWEEN THE TIGRIS AND EUPHRATES

There was no single country called Mesopotamia. The term is generally used to describe the area of land between the Tigris and Euphrates Rivers. From around 3500 B.C.E. the importance of different city-states rose and fell. In broadly chronological order, these city-states included Ur and Uruk, Sumer, Akkad, Babylon, and Assyria. The Mesopotamian period ended soon after 331 B.C.E., when Alexander the Great conquered the region. This book introduces the most important examples of the technologies invented and used by the various powers of ancient Mesopotamia.

The Gate of Ishtar was the entrance to the city of Babylon. It was dedicated to the city's main goddess.

TECHNICAL KNOW-HOW

The first people living in Mesopotamia were hunter–gatherers.

Mesopotamia has been called the "cradle of civilization." Many great technological advances were made there. Before the Mesopotamians, people lived as nomadic hunter–gatherers. They lived in caves and used basic stone tools. Their clothes were made from animal skins. They began living in round huts from around 10,000 B.C.E.

The Mesopotamians built the first cities. They used the seasonal flooding of the Euphrates and Tigris Rivers to create a network of canals and an irrigation system to water their crops. They used the mud from the rivers to make bricks for building and clay for pottery. They figured out that the bitumen (tar) that seeped out of the earth could be used as fuel in their kilns.

OUTGOING PEOPLES

The Mesopotamians invented technology for themselves, such as writing or using astronomy to develop a calendar. But they also interacted with other civilizations through trade, such as the Egyptians and Phoenicians. The Mesopotamians constantly exchanged ideas and learned from their neighbors who, in turn, learned from them.

HOUSE IN 4000 B.C.E

This house was built at Tell Madhhur in eastern Iraq.

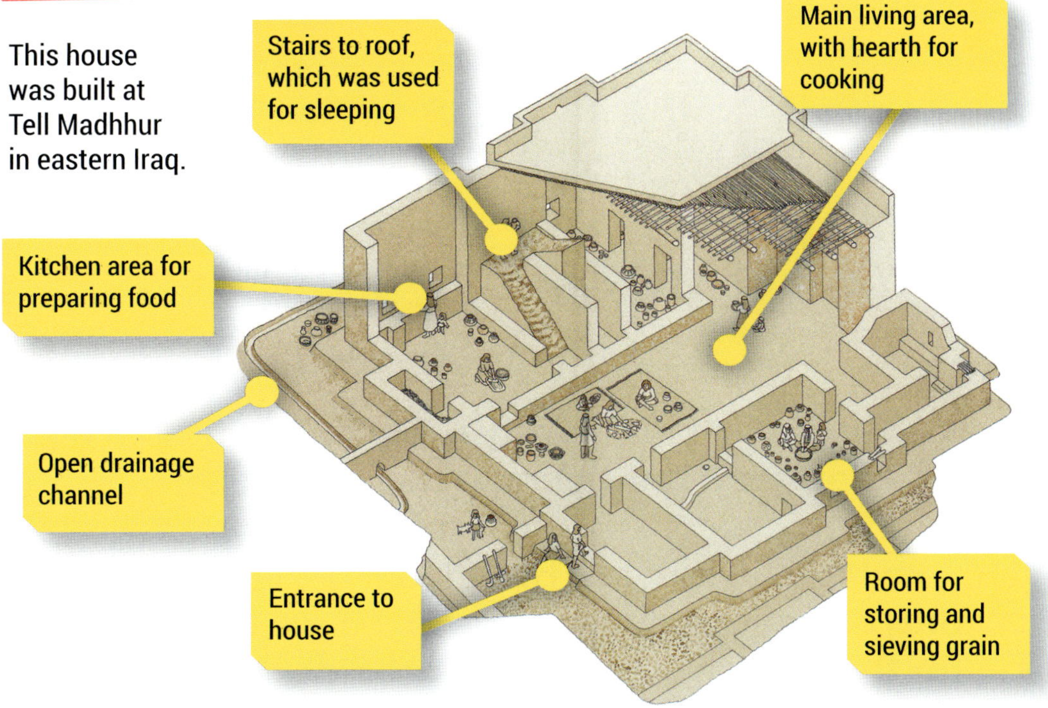

CANALS AND RIVERS

The Euphrates River runs through a barren landscape. When the river will flood is not as predictable as the Nile.

Mesopotamia literally means "the land between the rivers." The Tigris and Euphrates were used to water the land for farming. Cities were built from mud that was dug out of the riverbanks. But it was difficult for the Mesopotamians to predict when the rivers would flood.

Both rivers usually flooded between April and June. Sometimes, a huge flood altered a river's course and washed away villages. In other years, the flood did not happen at all. In the north, where it did not rain often, people saved river water by digging canals to collect it.

WATERWAYS

Workers built thousands of canals in the desert in order to collect and store water. They made raised earth banks near the rivers and diverted water into the channels. As the population grew, the network of canals expanded, but they regularly silted up. Workers cleared the silt with copper-bladed shovels, and carried it away in baskets made from reeds.

TECHNICAL SPECS

» The sources of the Euphrates and Tigris lie in the mountains of present-day Turkey.

» The banks of the Tigris River are steeper than those of the Euphrates River.

» The Tigris flows faster than the Euphrates, so less silt builds up in it.

» Silt raised the bed of the Euphrates so that it was higher than the nearby Tigris. At Babylon, water flowed from the Euphrates to the Tigris along a canal built through the city.

» The landscape of northern Mesopotamia was semiarid desert. Irrigation turned it into a region of marshes, mud flats, lagoons, and reed banks.

» Both rivers empty into the Persian Gulf.

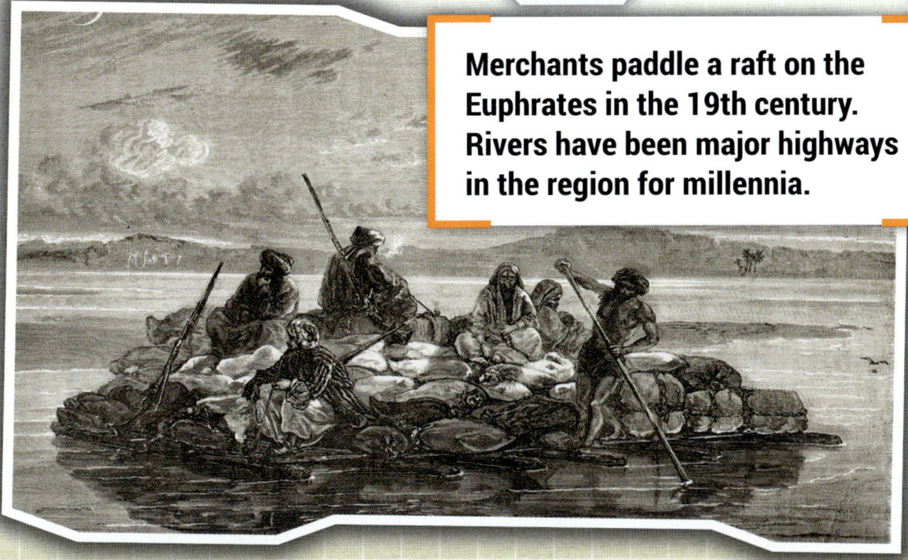

Merchants paddle a raft on the Euphrates in the 19th century. Rivers have been major highways in the region for millennia.

FARMING AND IRRIGATION

Rainfall was highest in the hilly regions near the borders of Mesopotamia. Farming began in these areas as early as 10,000 B.C.E. It only became possible to grow crops on the open plains in the middle of Mesopotamia when artificial irrigation was invented. Farmers were able to control the flow of water through a series of dams.

Barley was cut by hand using sickles.

Shadufs are still used in West Asia to lift water for irrigation. This illustration of a group of shadufs was drawn in the 19th century.

Early farmers used sticks and hoes to turn the soil. The wooden plow was invented in Mesopotamia around 3500 B.C.E. The plow transformed farming. Much larger areas of land could be prepared to grow crops such as barley.

IRRIGATION

Irrigation was controlled by a series of canals and mud banks. Water was lifted to the fields using a shaduf. This was a bucket attached to a pole that worked as a lever. The shaduf was invented in Mesopotamia before 2000 B.C.E. It was later adopted by the ancient Egyptians.

TECHNICAL SPECS

» Land close to the rivers was fertile and easy to farm. Further away, it was dry and uninhabited.

» The plow was invented in China around the same time as it was invented in Mesopotamia.

» Laws required that all Mesopotamians help repair canals or build new ones.

» Some canals were over 1,000 years old.

» Farmers harvested their crops with sickles.

» Popular crops were barley, onions, apples, grapes, and turnips.

» Salt was a major problem for farmers. Too much salt on the land meant crops failed.

WATER SUPPLIES

The Mesopotamians invented wooden waterwheels. In some areas, similar wheels are still used to power machinery.

Most water came from the two major rivers, the Tigris and Euphrates, and the network of canals. The major cities were therefore built close to these sources of water. Other cities relied on springs, wells, aqueducts, or cisterns. The Mesopotamians understood how important it was to have supplies of clean water.

In the city of Nimrud, wells were dug 90 feet (27.5 m) deep. The wells meant the city could have access to clean water if it was besieged. King Sennacherib built a stone aqueduct to carry water 6 miles (9.6 km) into Nineveh. It was fed by streams, so the city had a constant fresh water supply.

SEWAGE

Before 2000 B.C.E., royal palaces and the homes of the wealthy had indoor toilets. These were placed against an outside wall and consisted of a seat over a hole leading to a terracotta pipe. The pipe carried sewage to a river through a system of drains that ran beneath the streets.

TECHNICAL SPECS

» The well at Nimrud could provide 5,000 gallons of water a day.

» Water was pulled up from the bottom of the well using a chain of clay pots on a pulley wheel.

» The aqueduct at Nineveh was made from stone. Water flowed over its surface, which was made from hardened earth, waterproofed by bitumen, and lined with stone.

» A typical bathroom had a floor made from baked bricks waterproofed with bitumen. A seat hid the hole of the toilet, which was flushed using a jug of water.

» Waterwheels may have existed as early as 4000 B.C.E. They were the first machines to create mechanical energy without relying on energy from animals or humans.

An old village and mosque on the banks of the Euphrates River in what is now modern-day Turkey.

CLAY POTS

The Mesopotamian civilization could be said to have been built on clay. Mud from the banks of the major rivers was not only crafted into useful pots and containers, but also allowed the invention of writing and the building of great cities.

A potter makes a vessel from a coil of clay, which he will smooth together. Other vessels were made by pressing clay into molds.

A man rolls a cylinder seal over a clay tablet that will be tied to a storage jar to show who owns it.

The first Mesopotamians shaped clay pots by hand and left them to harden in the sun. Around 4500 B.C.E. they invented a potter's wheel. Around 2000 B.C.E. they invented a faster wheel rotated by foot. It meant pots could be made faster, and with thinner walls. From 1500 B.C.E. pots were glazed. That made them stronger and more waterproof, as well as being colorful and decorative.

BRICKS

The first mud bricks were made from clay mixed with straw to strengthen them. The bricks were dried in the sun. They were used to build homes and also the ziggurats that rose above the cities.

TECHNICAL SPECS

» Early pots were made from coils or slabs of clay smoothed together.

» The potter's wheel made the walls of pots more uniform in thickness, with fewer air bubbles, so they were less likely to break when they were fired.

» The Mesopotamians used sticks, bones, teeth, and shells to engrave pots before they dried.

» Before glazes were invented, potters rubbed the outside of pots with smooth stones to create a matte sheen.

» Glaze was applied with brushes made from animal hair.

CONSTRUCTION

Building in ancient Mesopotamia was dependent on available materials. There were few trees and little stone in the flat desert landscape, but there was lots of mud. There was also plenty of sunshine. Dried mud bricks became the most common material for the construction of homes and public buildings.

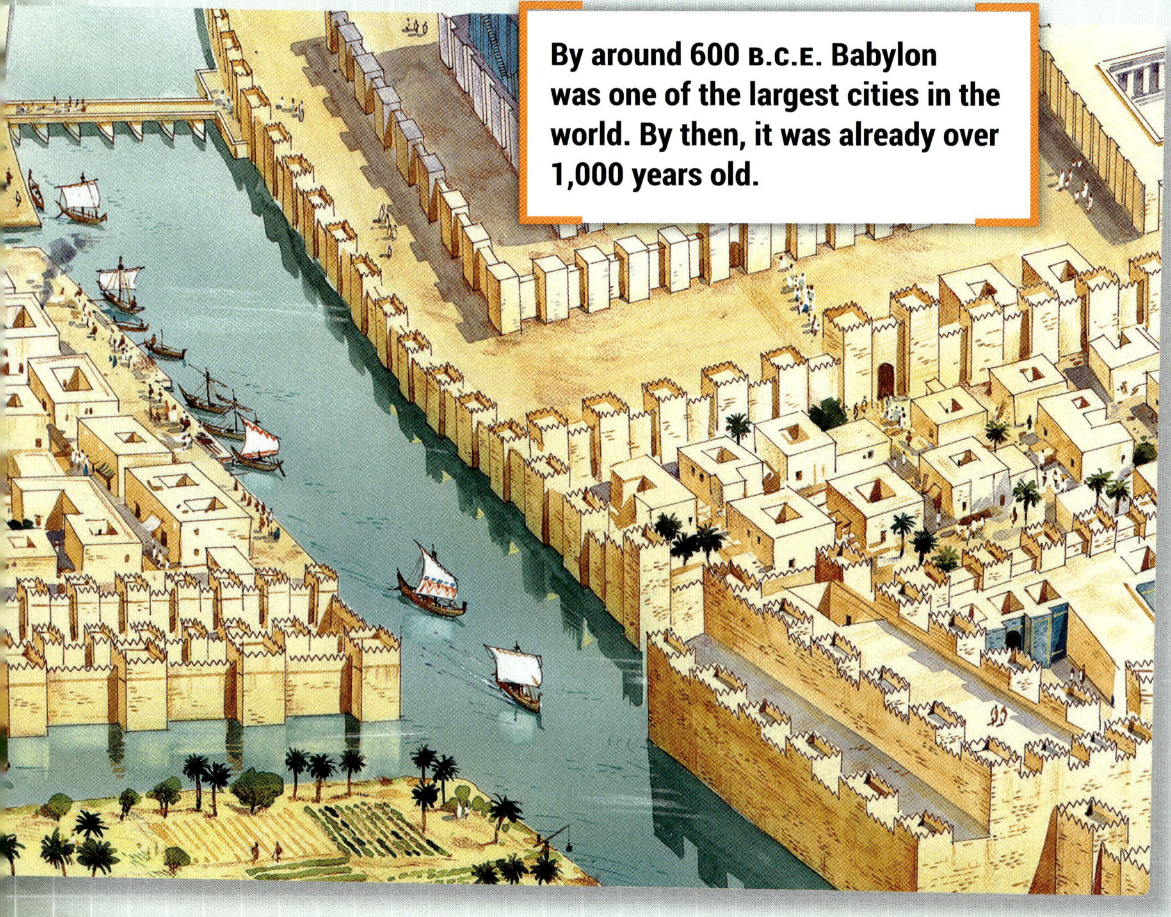

By around 600 B.C.E. Babylon was one of the largest cities in the world. By then, it was already over 1,000 years old.

TECHNICAL SPECS

» Mud bricks were made by hand. Workers molded mud mixed with chopped reeds or animal dung.

» Bricks were usually dried in the sun. Some bricks were fired in hot ovens to make them water resistant. These were used for public buildings, not homes.

» In the city of Ur, builders used naturally occurring bitumen as mortar to hold bricks together.

» Liquid mud was used both as mortar and as plaster for sealing and smoothing the walls.

» If wood was available, it was used for doors.

» Clay or stone were used to create drains and door frames.

BRICK

A worker's fingers have left imprints where he shaped the mud brick.

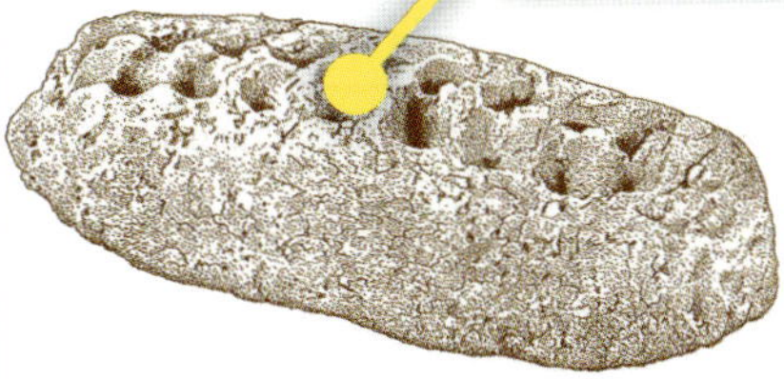

Mud is pressed into wooden molds to be dried as bricks. In the Americas, sun-dried bricks were called adobe.

The richer a person was, the bigger the house they built. The homes of the wealthy were three stories high and had many rooms. All houses had a thick outer wall of mud bricks. There were no outside windows. This helped to ensure privacy and also kept the house cool during the day.

HOME CONSTRUCTION

Inside the home, rooms were arranged around a central courtyard. This helped to keep the house cool. Roofs were made from the trunks of palm trees, if they were available. These beams were covered with a layer of reed and palm leaf matting that was coated with mud to seal and smooth it.

CITY LIFE

Although there had been cities before in places like Jericho and Catal Hüyuk, Mesopotamia was the first truly urban civilization. From around 4000 B.C.E., cities appeared throughout Mesopotamia and by 3450 B.C.E. much of the population lived in busy settlements surrounded by walls.

A market in the shadow of a ziggurat. Before coins were invented in the seventh century B.C.E., payment was usually made in corn.

The ruins of the ziggurat are all that remain of the ancient city of Ur. Other buildings have crumbled away.

People probably lived in cities because of the need for water. People had to cooperate to store water and irrigate the land, so they lived in groups. Before 3000 B.C.E., the Euphrates River changed course. Many villages were abandoned, and more people moved to the cities.

CITIES OF MUD

The first important city, Uruk, was built around 2700 B.C.E. Like other cities, it was protected by a wall of mud bricks. Each city had its own ruler and god, to whom the city's ziggurat was dedicated. People also sheltered there in times of flood.

TECHNICAL SPECS

» Uruk was divided into three zones: one-third was housing, one-third was for temples, and one-third was used for gardens.

» The ziggurat at Uruk was made from mud bricks with layers of reeds and matting between the brickwork layers.

» Most city streets were unpaved. They were used by people to dump trash and sewage. When the street was full of debris, the people covered it with another layer of mud. As the street level rose, people built steps to reach their doorways.

» Archaeologists in Uruk have discovered what seems to have been an early drainage system.

ZIGGURATS

Stepped, pyramid-shaped ziggurats rose high above the flat plains and dominated Mesopotamian cities. These buildings represented a sacred mountain and the design was later copied and adapted by other civilizations, such as the Egyptians. The first ziggurat was built around 2000 B.C.E.

The ziggurat of Ur has been re-created. Huge stone staircases led to the top of the ziggurat.

Hundreds of workers were involved in the construction of ziggurats.

Ziggurats were temples. The ancient Sumerians believed that powerful gods lived in the sky. They wanted to build tall structures to reach the heavens. They did not know how to build pyramids, so they built a series of stepped platforms.

FALSE MOUNTAIN

Ziggurats had a temple on top. Religious ceremonies were held there to honor the gods. The core of the building was made from mud bricks. To weatherproof the outside, burned bricks were used, held together with bitumen mortar. In times of flood, people sheltered in the ziggurats.

TECHNICAL SPECS

» The first ziggurat was built by Ur-Nammu, who ruled Ur from 2112–2095 B.C.E.

» Bitumen mortar was one of the great inventions of the Mesopotamians. It was made from bitumen—petroleum—that seeped out of the ground. This was the first use of oil in the Middle East.

» Ziggurats could be built with or without staircases.

» Ziggurats were built from a solid core of unfired mud bricks and an outer layer of fired bricks. The outer bricks were often glazed and colored.

» Terraces were filled with plants and trees in containers.

» Drains carried the water away from the upper levels.

BABYLON'S GARDENS

Babylon was the capital city of southern Mesopotamia. It was at the height of its power and fame in the sixth century B.C.E. Its Hanging Gardens were said to be one of the Seven Wonders of the Ancient World. Many people have tried to imagine what they might have looked like.

This is an illustration of how the Hanging Gardens might have appeared. No one knows what they really looked like.

The builders faced two technical problems. How were the plants watered? And how were the clay bricks kept dry?

SOLUTIONS

Archaeologists believe water was taken from the Euphrates River. A chain pump carried water to a pool at the top of the gardens. Gates opened to send the water into channels that watered the gardens. To stop the clay bricks from getting damp, the plants grew in containers lined with stone, reeds, bitumen, tiles, and lead. No water could seep out.

TECHNICAL SPECS

» The terraces were supported on arched vaults, or hollow spaces, held up by columns.

» Unusual for Mesopotamia, the gardens were said to be built using stone slabs.

» A chain pump was a series of buckets on a chain looped around two wheels. The bottom wheel sat in a pool of water. As it turned, the buckets dipped into the water and carried it to the upper wheel, where they tipped the water out.

» Some accounts describe how water was raised up the mountain by a mechanical device called an Archimedes screw, a spiral rotating inside a sloping tube.

HANGING GARDENS

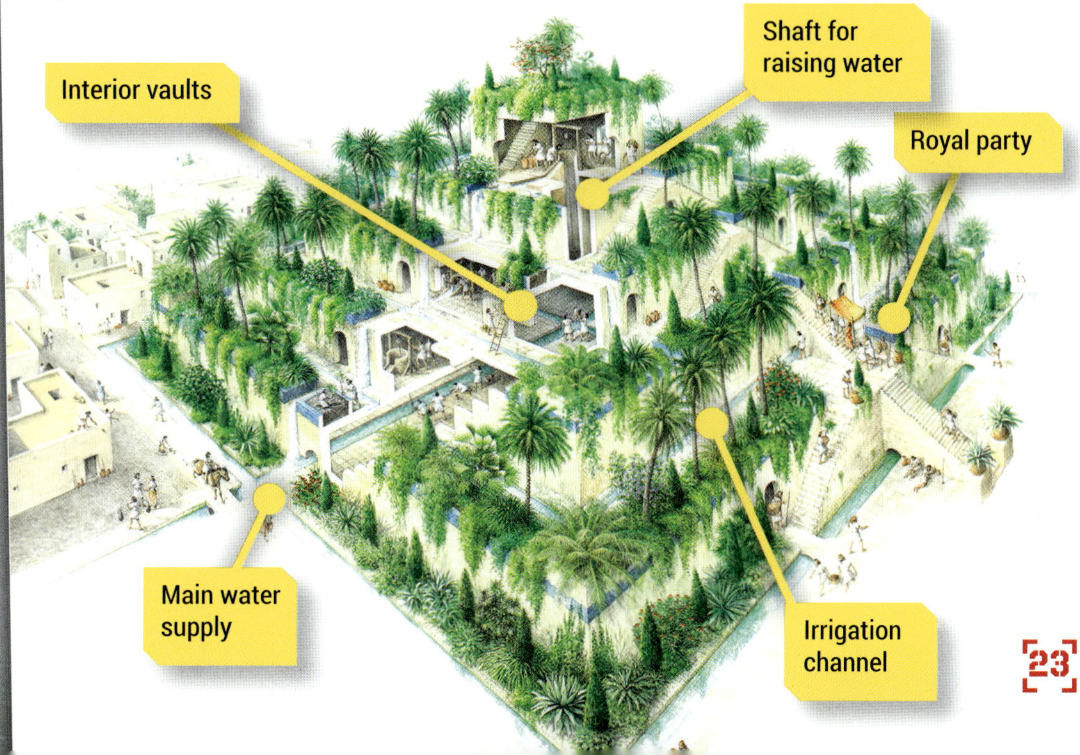

TRANSPORTATION

Roads were unpaved, so wheeled transport was not always practical. Sleds were used to pull heavy loads across the ground. The easiest way for people to move around Mesopotamia was by water. Boats sailed up and down the Tigris and Euphrates, and along the canals. Cargo ships sailed in the Red Sea, Indian Ocean, and Persian Gulf.

The Marsh Arabs of what is now Iraq still use boats made out of waterproofed reeds. They also use reeds to build their homes.

This is a reconstruction of a sled that was used by a queen of Ur. It was pulled over the ground by two oxen.

BOATBUILDING

Different boats were used for different purposes. For sea journeys, the Sumerians built boats out of wood. The Akkadians built two kinds of boat. The *quppu* was like a circular basket covered with animal hides. It was paddled on the Tigris River. The Akkadians also used a raft called a *kalakku*. It was made from bundles of reeds on top of inflated goatskins. It floated downriver with the current. When the boat reached its destination, the kalakku was dismantled. The skins were deflated and loaded on a donkey to travel back north so that they could be reused.

TECHNICAL SPECS

» To cross rivers and canals, people used floats made from reeds and inflated goatskins.

» To inflate a goatskin, the neck and three legs were tied tightly together. The swimmer blew into the fourth leg to keep it afloat.

» In the 18th century B.C.E., soldiers in the Assyrian army were issued with goatskin floats to cross rivers and canals.

» On land, porters, donkeys, and mules transported goods. Local trips were made in wheeled carts.

» Boats from the Royal Cemetery at Ur (about 2600 B.C.E.) were the same shape as the reed boats used by the Marsh Arabs of southern Iraq today.

THE WHEEL

The first wheels in history were probably potters' wheels. It is thought they were invented in ancient Sumeria in around 4500 to 3300 B.C.E. Wheels for transport were probably introduced in ancient Mesopotamia in around 3200 B.C.E. Many experts think the use of a wheel rotating around a fixed axle is one of the defining features of a civilization.

FIRST WHEELS

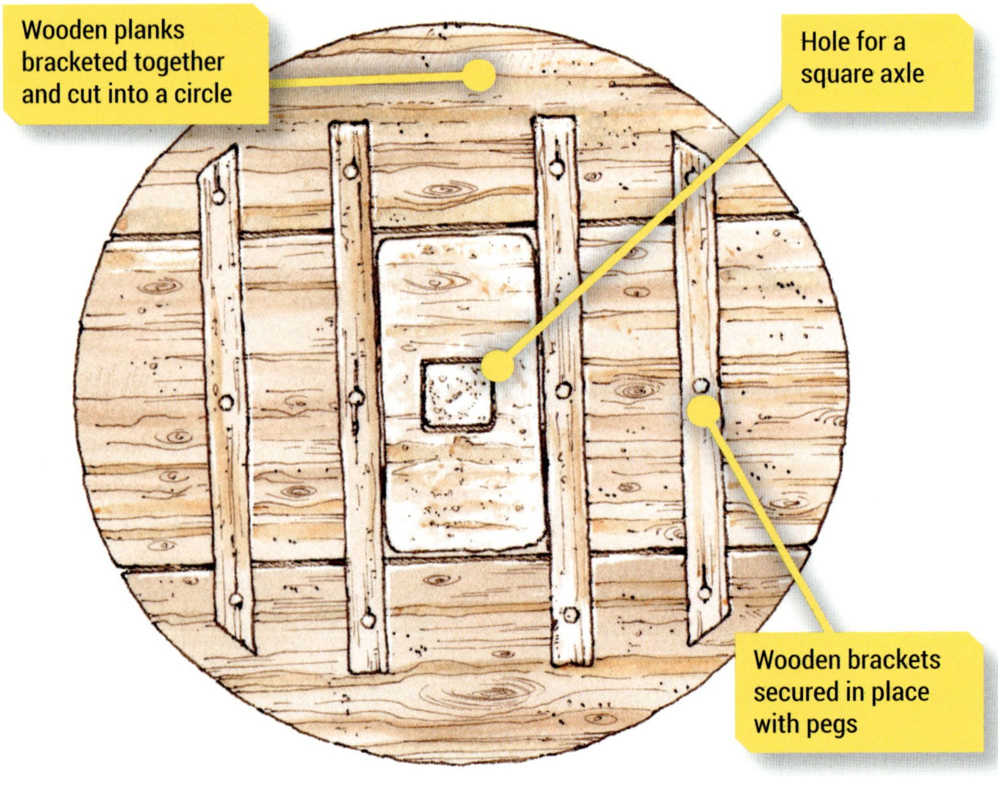

Early potters' wheels were turned by hand. The wheel spun slowly, so the walls of pots were quite thick.

TECHNICAL SPECS

» Wheel technology was used in potters' wheels and, from the first century B.C.E., in the waterwheel.

» The transportation wheel may have been based on the logs used to roll sledges carrying loads. As the object moved forward, the log rollers were taken from behind the load and put in front of it again.

» The tall trees needed to make rollers and wheels were not common in ancient Mesopotamia. No one knows where the wood came from.

» The ancient Egyptians took Mesopotamian wheel technology and improved upon it.

As early as 3200 B.C.E., the Sumerians of Mesopotamia made pictures of carts with solid wheels. The wheels were made from two pieces of wooden plank, bracketed together and cut into a circular shape. Wooden axles passed through the center of the circle and were held in place by linchpins. The Sumerians used this kind of wheel for war chariots.

ADAPTABLE ARENA

By 2000 B.C.E. the Sumerians had invented spoked wheels. Spokes joined the axle to an outer wheel rim. This made chariots much lighter and therefore easier to maneuver.

THE NIGHT SKY AND ASTROLOGY

From the second millennium B.C.E., priests studied the night sky and noted the position of the planets and stars and the phases of the moon. From their observations of the skies, the Mesopotamians worked out a calendar. They also created the first zodiac, which was based on groups of stars called constellations. The ancient Mesopotamians believed they could tell what would happen in the future if they watched the skies.

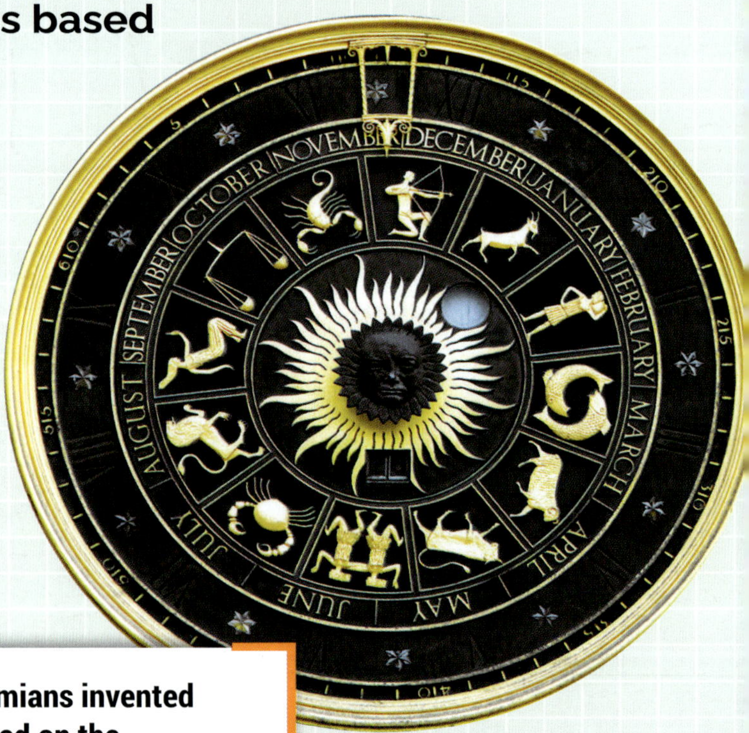

The Mesopotamians invented the zodiac based on the constellations. They used the zodiac to try to predict the future.

From studying the moon, Sumerian astronomers worked out a lunar calendar. Later, the Babylonians predicted events such as eclipses, which they thought were bad omens. Assyrian astronomers compiled a list of the positions of the stars.

THE ZODIAC

Careful observation of the skies led to the invention of the zodiac. This marked a change from compiling predictions for the king or state to predicting the future of the individual. By the fifth century B.C.E., the circular zodiac belt had been created, with 12 signs. Each sign occupied 30 degrees of the 360 degrees of the circle.

TECHNICAL SPECS

» Astronomical tablets found in Nineveh date from 700 B.C.E.

» The Sumerian calendar had 12 months of 30 days. To balance the 360-day lunar calendar with the 365.25-day solar year, they added extra days every three years.

» A Sumerian cuneiform tablet from 4000 B.C.E. describes the sighting of an exploding star.

» The first known baby horoscope was cast for a child born on April 29, 410 B.C.E.

» Assyrian astronomers used tubes as viewfinders and measured time with water clocks and sundials.

» An eclipse obscured by clouds was not seen as a bad omen.

Mesopotamians believed there was a direct link between the heavens and what happened on Earth.

WRITING

Cuneiform means wedge-shaped. It refers to the shape of the marks made in the clay.

Perhaps the most important invention in the ancient world was the creation of writing. An early form of writing first appeared in Sumer. The Sumerians needed to keep records of their cattle, sheep, and crops. From 3300 B.C.E. they began to draw simple pictures on soft clay tablets. A bull's head represented cattle, and an ear of barley stood for grain.

The early pictures changed into curved lines and then into cuneiform. These wedge-shaped characters were easy to press into clay. Around 3100 B.C.E., people began using signs to stand for sounds as well as for objects. This was the real beginning of writing.

FIRST ALPHABET

Between 1700 and 1500 B.C.E., the first alphabet appeared in ancient Palestine and Syria. The Mesopotamians created a cuneiform alphabet around 1000 B.C.E. There were more than 600 cuneiform signs. Originally used for record keeping, writing was soon also used for stories, laws, spells, and recipes.

TECHNICAL SPECS

» The earliest known examples of writing date from 3300 B.C.E. They were found on clay tablets from Uruk.

» The early writing system had more than 700 different signs.

» Clay tablets were put inside a clay "envelope," so they could not be tampered with.

» Cuneiform could be read from left to right or top to bottom, depending on how it was written.

» Merchants used cylinder seals to imprint a design on soft clay to show that goods or transactions were genuine.

The Mesopotamians had plenty of clay for tablets and they made wedge-shaped "pens" from reed stems.

COUNTING, WEIGHTS, AND MEASURES

The Mesopotamians developed two counting systems. One had symbols for singles, tens, and hundreds. This is the system we still use today. The Sumerians introduced a base 60 system (sexagesimal). It is the origin for the division of 60 for hours and angles. The Mesopotamians also had units of weight, length, and volume.

Duck-shaped weights were used to measure quantities. When corn was used as money, it had to be weighed.

Numbers greater than 10 were first used in Mesopotamia around 3000 B.C.E. (numerals were first used in Egypt around 3400 B.C.E.). The Mesopotamians pressed numbers into wet clay with reed pens. They used Pythagoras's theorem to work out the area of triangles 1,000 years before Pythagoras lived. Base 60 was used to calculate a 360-degree circle, as well as minutes and seconds.

TECHNICAL SPECS

- Surviving clay tablets contain students' exercises in calculation, plus multiplication tables.
- The Mesopotamians did not use zero.
- An hour was divided into 60 minutes and a minute into 60 seconds.
- The day was divided into 12 hours of daylight and 12 hours of night (each was one-fifth of 60).
- The Babylonian mile was the equivalent of 7 miles (11 km).

COMMON WEIGHTS

Weights were standardized in the city of Ur in around 2000 B.C.E. Granite weights, in the shape of a duck, were used by merchants and buyers to ensure that the goods they were buying and selling were of a standard size. They placed the ducks on one side of a balance with the goods on the other.

The Mesopotamians used a simple balance. Whatever was being weighed was put on one side, and a weight was put on the other.

WARFARE AND WEAPONS

The first record of warfare in Mesopotamia was around 2500 B.C.E. City-states fought over water and farmland, and walls were built around the cities to protect them. In the early days, soldiers were slaves and citizens. The Akkadians had the first professional army.

This wall carving shows Assyrian archers and spear carriers defending a city from the top of its walls.

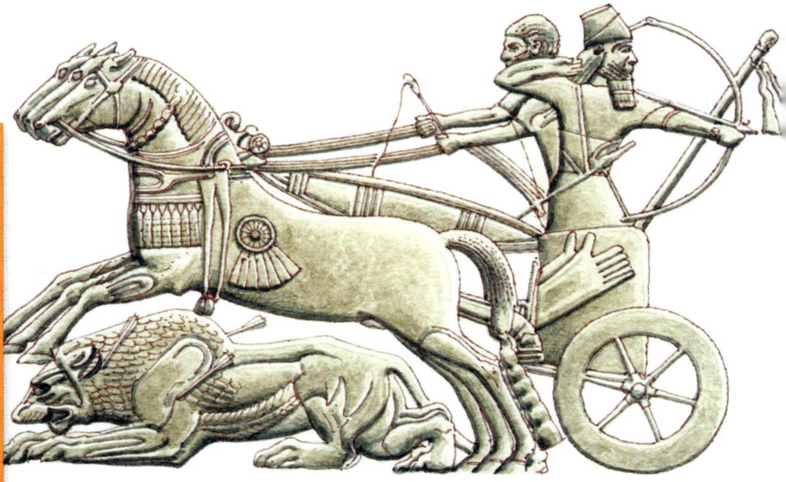

This illustration shows a chariot pulled by two horses as an archer takes aim. The chariot allowed archers to get closer to the enemy.

Early weapons were based on hunting weapons, and were made from wood and stone. By 4000 B.C.E., copper was being used to make axes, spears, and daggers. Bronze weapons appeared around 2000 B.C.E. and iron weapons 1,000 years later.

SIEGES

Cities defended themselves with city walls. To defeat enemy cities, armies used siege weapons, such as battering rams and siege towers, from about 1000 B.C.E. Around 1500 B.C.E., the first two-wheeled, horse-drawn war chariots were used. They revolutionized warfare.

TECHNICAL SPECS

» Horses were used 4,000 years ago to carry military equipment.

» Soldiers wore armor made from tiny overlapping pieces of bronze, like scales, sewn on to a tunic.

» The Assyrians introduced cavalry units. They rode bareback, as the saddle had not been invented at that point.

» The Assyrian army had up to 50,000 troops, most of whom were infantry or foot soldiers.

» Chariots were manned by a charioteer and an archer.

» Sargon the Great of Akkad (2335–2279 B.C.E.) was the first ruler to properly train and equip an army of professional soldiers.

CRAFTS

Craftspeople in Mesopotamia were free citizens who made fine pottery, glassware, gold and silver jewelry, woven textiles, ivory figurines, and other goods that were traded. They brought wealth to the cities. Stone and metal were often imported, but the Mesopotamians had a ready supply of bitumen to heat their kilns to bake raw materials into lasting objects.

This golden calf mosaic from Assyria was made from glazed clay tiles.

TECHNICAL SPECS

» Glass was worked into shape before it cooled and hardened. It was rolled into sheets, turned into tubes, or pressed into molds.

» In stone reliefs, figures were carved according to importance. The king was always bigger than his courtiers, who were bigger than everyone else.

» Statues and reliefs were finished with semiprecious stones, such as lapis lazuli for blue eyes.

» Jewelers beat leaf metal into thin strips and added stones such as agate and jasper. Such imported stones were highly valued.

This ornate ribbed glass vessel comes from Ur. It was glazed with different-colored abstract decorations.

Cuneiform records say that glass was made during Sumerian times. In fact, no glass has been found from earlier than 1500 B.C.E. However, as early as the fourth and third millennia B.C.E., Mesopotamians experimented with chemicals such as lime soda and silicates. Mixing those with minerals led to the discovery of brightly colored glass. Craftspeople used glass to make containers, beads, small figures, and parts of statues.

STONE CARVING

The Mesopotamians were skilled carvers. They carved statues of their gods and goddesses out of marble and limestone. The Assyrians carved stone reliefs for their palaces. These stone pictures usually showed figures in profile and depicted rituals and mythological scenes.

METALS

Mesopotamia was rich in mud, reeds, palm, fish, and grain. They had few deposits of metals, but metals were very important, so the ancient Mesopotamians had to trade for them. They imported ores from which they could extract metals. This led to long-distance trade with other ancient civilizations, such as the peoples of the Indus Valley.

Copper did occur naturally in Mesopotamia. As early as the fourth millennium B.C.E, craftsmen extracted copper from other metals to make objects. The copper may have come from the Timna Valley in the south.

This helmet was made from silver and gold. The silver was dissolved so that the surface looked like gold.

Most copper objects were a mixture, or alloy, of copper and arsenic. The alloy was easier to cast and harder than pure copper. Copper was popular up to sometime before 3000 B.C.E., when the Sumerians learned how to make bronze.

BRONZE

The Sumerians made bronze by adding tin to copper. Bronze had a lower melting point, so it was easier to cast in different shapes. It was also stronger, so it was good for tools and weapons. Objects were also made from imported gold, silver, and lead. They invented the "lost wax" process for casting statues, arrowheads, tools, and other more complex weapons.

TECHNICAL SPECS

- Blades for knives were made by carving into the face of a flat stone. Copper was heated and poured into the stone mold, where it cooled and was then removed.
- Furnaces were similar to the kilns used to fire pottery.
- Workers used bellows made from animal skin to pump air into the furnaces. This made the fire burn hotter so that copper could be melted and poured as liquid metal.
- Fuel for the furnaces was provided by the bitumen that seeped out of the ground.
- The Mesopotamians used silver to make an early form of money. These tokens, called "shekels," were not coins, but ingots of a standard weight.

HOW TO ...

In the "lost wax" process, a model is made out of wax, then packed in clay to make a mold. The mold is heated so the wax melts and drains through holes. Molten, or liquid, metal is poured into the mold, filling the space left by the "lost wax." It is then left to cool and harden. The clay is broken open to reveal the new object.

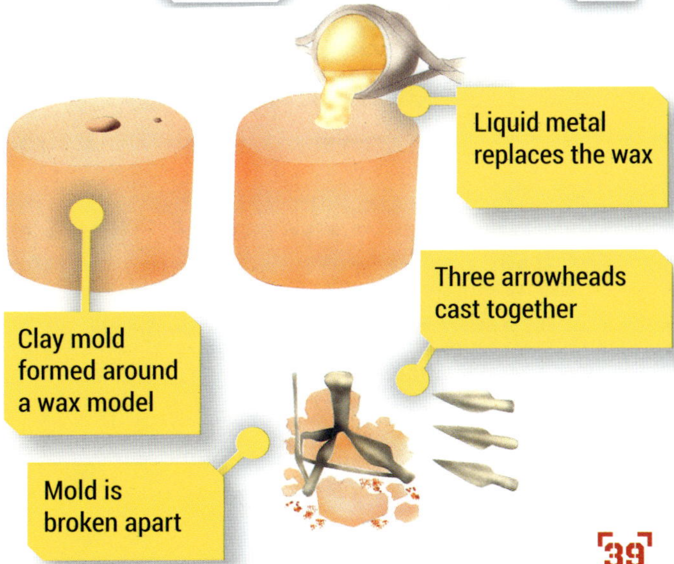

SPINNING AND WEAVING

Early peoples in Mesopotamia went from wearing animal skins to wearing handwoven garments. These were often finished with embroidery and appliqué. Spinning and the weaving and dyeing of cloth became a major industry. The main fabrics used were wool and linen.

Ancient hand looms were used to weave cloth for clothes and blankets.

In Sumer, people plucked sheep for their wool; later they started to shear them. Men often wore belted sheepskins that came to their ankles; women wore a toga-like garment.

SPINNING

Women spun and wove flax to make linen. They did this on flat looms until upright looms were introduced. These had ceramic weights to keep the yarn tight. Textiles were often dyed with colors using animal, plant, or mineral extracts.

TECHNICAL SPECS

- Linen was used only for high-quality garments worn by priests, or to be placed on statues of gods.
- Felt was made from pressed low-quality wool or goat hair. It was used to make shoes.
- By the third millennium B.C.E., the Mesopotomians invented the vertical loom.
- In the eighth century B.C.E. rulers in Nimrud were buried with cloth decorated with appliqué, or pieces of another cloth sewn on.
- No word for "tailor" existed before the neo-Babylonian period. This may mean that making clothes was only seen as a special skill late in Mesopotamian history.

A scribe keeps account of textiles and other goods for trade.

MEDICINE

Cuneiform tablets from the library of Ashurbanipal, the last Assyrian king of Nineveh, reveal that the Mesopotamian medical profession was relatively well developed by 1500 B.C.E. Practitioners knew about sickness and had ways of treating the sick. The tablets describe two kinds of doctor: the asipu and the asu.

Priests use spells to try to cure a patient. They are dressed as fish so they can appeal to the god of water.

The asipu used magic to treat sick people. Early Mesopotamians believed sickness was caused by committing a sin. Asipus tried to expel demons by using charms and spells. If they could not cure the illness, the asu tried his herbal remedies.

EVIDENCE OF SURGERY

Later, Mesopotamians realized that illness could be caused by things such as rotten food or too much alcohol. One 5,000-year-old skeleton shows that the person had surgery to remove part of his skull, perhaps in order to relieve the symptoms of a headache.

TECHNICAL SPECS

» Mesopotamian religion banned the dissection of corpses.

» Doctors believed that emotions were located in the liver and intelligence in the heart.

» The first set of laws, the Code of Hammurabi (1700 B.C.E.), punished surgical mistakes by mutilation or death.

» The oldest medical text was written in 2100 B.C.E.

» Some remedies were related to the color of the disease: Jaundice was treated with yellow medicine.

» One medical record lists 230 remedies. It describes a mixture of herbs and perhaps beetroot, cilantro, and parsley that was drunk or applied externally.

» After the Mesopotamians, medical knowledge stood still for 2,000 years, until the ancient Greeks.

This tablet lists medical prescriptions and magic spells against poisoning. It describes how a mixture of mustard, nuts, grain, thyme, and other plants should be smeared onto the skin in order to cure the patient.

TIMELINE

B.C.E.

c.5000 Farmers move from northern Mesopotamia to the flat plains of the south.

c.4000 Southern settlements begin to grow into towns, such as Ur.

c.3500 The first Mesopotamian towns grow into cities, with dense housing, royal palaces, and large temples.

c.3100 Cuneiform writing appears at Uruk.

c.3000 Metalworkers mix copper and tin to make bronze, which is used for tools and weapons.

c.3000 The wheel is invented in Mesopotamia.

c.2750 Under the First Dynasty of Ur, the city of Ur begins a period of dominance that will last over 250 years.

c.2500 Two Mesopotamian city-states, Lagash and Umma, fight the first war on record.

c.2330 Sumer is conquered by King Sargon, the ruler of Akkad.

c.2113 King Ur-Nammu founds the Third Dynasty of Sumer and throws off the rule of the foreign Gutians, who have conquered Sumer and Akkad.

c.2095 The throne of Ur passes to King Shulgi, who builds the city's Great Ziggurat.

c.2000 Ur is overthrown by the Elamites, from the east.

c.2000 Weapons are made from bronze.

c.1900 A desert people known as the Amorites conquer a large part of Mesopotamia; they make Babylon their capital.

c.1792 King Hammurabi comes to the throne in Babylon. He takes over Sumer and Akkad, as well as part of Assyria.

c.1783 Ur is attacked and destroyed by the Babylonians.

c.1600 Much of Mesopotamia is conquered by foreign peoples, the Hittites and the Kassites.

c.1570 The Kassites found a dynasty that will rule Babylon for nearly 500 years.

c.1500 Two-wheeled war chariots are invented.

c.1500 The first-known glass is made in Mesopotamia.

c.1000 The Mesopotamians begin making iron weapons.

c.1000 The Mesopotamians develop their own alphabet, based on that of the Phoenicians.

c.950 The Assyrians of northern Mesopotamia begin a campaign of conquest that will eventually create a large empire in Mesopotamia and what is now Turkey.

c.612 Babylon rises to power again after the fall of the Assyrian empire. The new power is referred to as Neo-Babylonian, or "new Babylonian."

605 Nebuchadnezzar II comes to the throne in Babylon. He builds the city's famous Hanging Gardens. He also expands the Neo-Babylonian empire, conquering Syria, Palestine, and Jerusalem.

539 The Persian ruler Cyrus the Great conquers the Babylonian empire.

331 The Macedonian Alexander the Great overthrows the Persian empire and takes over Mesopotamia.

GLOSSARY

bitumen A substance related to petroleum that was used as a fuel and as a kind of waterproof tar.

canal An artificial waterway.

cast To pour molten metal into a mold and allow it to harden.

chariot A fast, two-wheeled, horse-drawn vehicle, used in warfare.

city-state A political unit ruled by a powerful city.

cuneiform Meaning "wedge-shaped," word used to describe writing in which characters were pressed with a wedge-shaped nib into soft clay.

cylinder seal A carved stone tube that was rolled over soft clay to leave a design that identified the owner.

eclipse When one heavenly body prevents the light from another heavenly body from reaching the Earth.

empire A large territory ruled by an emperor or empress.

glaze A thin, glassy covering put on clay to make it shiny.

hemp A plant whose fibers are used to make material.

horoscope An attempt to tell the future based on the movement of the planets and stars.

irrigation Artificially watering fields to enable crops to grow.

kiln A very hot oven used to harden pottery or bake bricks.

linchpin A pin at the end of an axle to stop a wheel from falling off as it turns.

siege engine A large machine used to attack the walls of a besieged city.

theorem A mathematical idea that has been demonstrated to be true.

vault An arched structure that forms a ceiling or roof.

ziggurat A tall building or temple that rose in a series of stories, each one smaller than the one below it.

zodiac A circular band that contains 12 astrological signs.

FURTHER RESOURCES

BOOKS

Captivating History. *Ancient Mesopotamia: A Captivating Introduction to the Rise and Fall of Mesopotamia.* Captivating History, 2022.

Captivating History. *Mesopotamian Cities: A Captivating Guide to Eridu, Uruk, Ur, Akkad, Assur, Lagash, Babylon, Nippur, Nimrud, and Nineveh.* Captivating History, 2022.

Levy, Janey. *The Advances of Ancient Mesopotamia* (That's Ancient!). Gareth Stevens, 2021.

Randolph, Joanne. *Living and Working in Ancient Mesopotamia* (Back in Time). Enslow Pub Inc, 2017.

Rodger, Ellen. *Ancient Mesopotamia Inside Out* (Ancient Worlds Inside Out). Crabtree Publishing, 2017.

WEBSITES

www.dkfindout.com/uk/history/mesopotamia/
An introduction to the land, culture, and technology of Ancient Mesopotamia.

sunearthday.nasa.gov/2006/locations/babylon.php
Page on Babylonian astronomy from the NASA program Sun–Earth Day.

www.mesopotamia.co.uk/staff/resources/background/bg07/home.html
British Museum teachers' page about Mesopotamian technology.

www.anciv.info/mesopotamia/
Ancient Civilizations guide to Mesopotamia, including technology.

Publisher's note to educators and parents: Our editors have carefully reviewed these websites to ensure that they are suitable for students. Many websites change frequently, however, and we cannot guarantee that a site's future contents will continue to meet our high standards of quality and educational value. Be advised that students should be closely supervised whenever they access the Internet.

INDEX